Passive income 009:

Proven steps to financial freedom

By

Leonardo M. Wright

Copyright © by Leonardo M. Wright 2022. All rights reserved.

Before this document is duplicated or reproduced in any manner, the publisher's consent must be gained. Therefore, the contents within can neither be stored electronically, transferred, nor kept in a database. Neither in Part nor full can the document be copied, scanned, faxed, or retained without approval from the publisher or creator.

Table of Contents

- Introduction 4
- Meaning and the misconception of passive income 7
- Risks of living on one income 11
- Nine most lucrative ways you could provide value and earn passively .. 18
- Reasons many struggle at building streams of passive income 88
- What it takes to create passive income business 101
- Conclusion 107

Introduction

"If you don't find a way to make money while you sleep, you'll work until you die" a statement once made by warren Buffet.

Now more than ever, there are several online and offline opportunities for people to generate passive income. But one of the main problems we have today from some of the books and videos on how to earn passively is a lack of honesty. They trick you into thinking it's a get-rich-quick scheme. They want you to believe making passive income is fast and easy and that you can make hundreds of thousands of dollars every year without putting in effort and providing value, which is almost impossible.

There are more than a hundred ways to earn passively but in this book, we'll cover nine potential passive income streams. For each of those, we are also going to talk about how difficult it is to get started, how difficult it is to make $100 per month from it, and how difficult it is to maintain it once you have created the thing in the first place. These nine distinct sources collectively bring in over $25,000 in weekly revenue for me and the company I run.

These days, with varying degrees of passiveness, it has taken me around eight years to build up, so you shouldn't expect to achieve those sorts of figures when you first start. I wished I had this book available when I initially started along the road to gaining financial freedom many years ago.

Meaning and the misconception of passive income

I usually put "passive income" in quotation marks when I talk about it since there is no such thing as "passive income" in reality. There is no method to generate income without engaging in any kind of activity at all. To clarify, when I refer to "passive income," I am referring to money that does not require us to actively work. So, let's assume you decided to create a book; if you write a book, publish the book, and the book is now available for purchase, then the effort has been completed successfully. After you have written and published the book, you will get royalties for each copy sold; this type of revenue is known as passive income. Because you've made something that now exists in the world and brings in money for you, you may be earning money even while you're getting some shut-eye.

The other aspect of passive income is that it takes a long time to get going. As a result, if you see any book before this one talking about how to get rich quick by some scheme, or if you see people in the reviews pretending to be me and saying things like "Oh my God, here's how you can get rich quick with crypto let's have this number," know that it is all a scam.

Passive income always takes a very long time to get going. That is not how it works at all. There is no easy method to get wealth quickly. It is not a thing; therefore, if you are searching for a get-rich-fast scheme, those things just don't exist, so you may as well not even try. Since it is not a thing, it is best to avoid trying to find one.

Since money is merely a medium for exchanging value, the only way to make money is to provide value. Please do not attempt to join a get-rich-quick scheme, as they do not exist; the only way to earn passive income is to create value in a way that is not primarily dependent on your time. Money is merely a medium for the exchange of value. Individuals who have attempted signing up for a get-rich-fast crypto scam or a gambling plan for "hey, here is how you sort of play poker online" have sent me many emails over the years. None of these things ever work, even though I've received many letters from these people. In the end, people always end up losing money, and the only way to gain money is to provide value to other people.

Risks of living on one income

Even in well-paying work, there is no guarantee of security. Be wise and diversify your income, said Ray Higdon. "Never rely on a single income," said Warren Buffet, one of the world's greatest billionaires. The ability to generate several sources of income is no longer a luxury; it is now a must. Building your revenue strength is the first stage in developing your financial stability.

Nobody's job is secure if the high unemployment rate and continuing job losses have taught us anything. Unfortunately, the majority of individuals depend only on their jobs for cash, which may be a dangerous way of life. You need to have enough financial security so that you lose track of when payday comes. Why don't you have residual revenues when you have residual bills?

Many people have been on a road of financial anguish and uncertainty as a result of our traditional professional route. The process is as follows: You choose a career, rise in that position, earn even better pay, and then, ideally, retire with a pension plan. Millions of individuals now go that route, depending on a single source of income, but given the current economic climate, that strategy is fundamentally wrong. If you rigorously adhere to it, you could be setting yourself up for tough financial times, longer work stretches before retirement, and in some circumstances, complete financial collapse.

There is enough evidence to demonstrate that families that rely only on one source of income are most in danger of falling into poverty. Your only source of money shouldn't be your paycheck. One of the most enduring methods to strengthen your financial basis is to supplement your primary income. JOB, according to someone once, stands for Just Over Broke. One school of thinking holds that having only one source of income would leave us perpetually in debt.

I came across a text in my attempt to provide a biblical justification for the notion of having numerous sources of income that is worth careful consideration. The principle of having several sources of income is concisely expressed by King Solomon in Ecclesiastes 11:2 (NIV translation) when he says, "Invest in seven endeavors, yes, in eight; for you know not what tragedy may fall upon the country." A millionaire typically has seven sources of income.

In the twenty-first century, there are several resources available for building different revenue streams. More than ever, we have access to information, people, and opportunities. Unfortunately, instead of causing a disturbance, individuals exploit all of these as a type of distraction. You possess the ability, timeframe, aptitude, and skills necessary to establish various revenue sources. The more revenue streams you can generate, the wealthier and more stable your financial situation will be.

"Never put all your eggs in one basket," you ask. Being reliant on a single source of income is perilous since it puts all of your eggs in one basket. Having a backup revenue source in case one fails is essential to maintaining cash flow.

The wealthiest persons are those who have many sources of income. Bill Gates, Jeff Bezos, Richard Branson, Elon Musk, Aliko Dangote, and Mark Zuckerberg all began with a single revenue stream, but over time, they expanded their companies to satisfy a variety of demands.

The belief that earning an additional source of money requires devoting the time and effort required for a second full-time job to a different profession is the main barrier keeping many individuals from adding other sources of income to their lives. Simply said, it is untrue. While working at your current employment, you may generate additional revenue. Simply being more digital, adaptable, strategic, and dynamic will suffice.

Nine most lucrative ways you could provide value and earn passively

Stocks and shares investment

Within the parameters of this discussion, the method by which we contribute value is by putting up our money. Offering money and investing in a service is a way of giving value. As a result, when we give a firm our money by buying their stocks, we get some kind of return for the investment we have made in that company.

We are starting with this because investing in stocks is the easiest way to make any passive income if you have any savings because having your money just sit in a savings account earning 0.01% interest doesn't do much for you. In contrast, if you had those savings and put them in stocks, you could be earning passive income from the money that is otherwise just sitting there. This is why we are starting with this.

Now that I'm in possession of it, I have a book titled "The full guide to stocks and shares investing for beginners." This book serves as an introduction to stocks and explains how they function in detail. If you're interested in this topic, I strongly suggest getting the book for a more in-depth understanding.

All the money I have in stocks and shares is put into index funds because I am not a financial counselor. This is the most basic strategy that I follow. When you invest, let's say, $1000 in the S&P 500, it essentially means that your $1000 is dispersed among the top 500 largest corporations in the United States. An index fund is comparable to the S&P 500 and is comparable to something like the S&P 500. Apples would make up 2% of the total if their sizes were considered, as you know. 2% in Facebook, 2% in Google, and 2% in Microsoft; after that, you probably won't have heard of the 500th firm on the list; nevertheless, if you wind up investing in any of the large U.S. corporations that you are familiar with, you will end up investing in all of them.

Therefore, if you are interested in getting started, you must register with a stockbroker. You can use Weebly if you're in the United States; if you're in the United Kingdom, you can use free trade or vanguard instead. Simply Google the term "best stock broker platform, your country name," and you should be able to locate a solution that meets your requirements, regardless of the nation in which you now reside. Because purchasing shares in an index fund is a simple process, our well-known evaluation methodology will only provide a one-star grade to the level of effort involved in getting started with this side hustle. Only one out of every five.

Getting started in the stock market is a relatively simple process.

Challenges

How challenging is generating a monthly income of $100 by purchasing stocks and shares? This, however, is contingent upon the general success of the stock market. Over the last year, the S&P 500 index has increased considerably, with a rise of over fifty percent since the beginning of 2021. Despite COVID and everything else that has been going on, it has increased by a significant 50%. Therefore, if you had invested $2,400 in the S&P 500 in April 2020, the fact that it has increased by 50% means that you would have made

$100 a month. This is not the best method to approach the situation, though, as you are well aware that things can go both ways and that the stock market performs differently depending on the time frame you are considering. As a result, this perspective is incorrect. If we take an average of the returns over the past thirty to fifty years, the S&P 500 has had around a ten-point-something percent return, which indicates that throughout the long run, it has increased by approximately ten percent year on average. This is not adjusted for inflation, in case there are any economists among us. So if we do some back-of-the-envelope calculations, we find that If we wish to invest in stocks and shares to earn $100 each month passively, To get a return of 10% on our investment in the S&P 500, we would need to have around $12,000., which is $1,200 a year and $100 a month. Consequently, we would have to put down $12,000.

If you invested $7,500 in the S&P 500 and left it there for five years without touching it, you would have made around $100 each month at the end of the fifth year. I discuss this scenario in further detail in my book on stocks. If we use this relatively typical rate of 10% per year, or if you put $5,000 in the S&P 500, then after ten years, you would be generating

$100 per month in income that was completely passive if you did nothing but let it sit there. Again, let's assume that's the standard 10%.

To answer the question, "How difficult is it to make $100 per month in passive income from stocks and shares?" the answer to this question kind of just depends on how difficult it is for you to save $5,000, $7,500, or $12,000 and then invest those savings in an index fund that tracks the U.S. stock market. Importantly, this is money you shouldn't need to touch for at least the next five to ten years, so the question boils down to how simple it is for them to create that kind of money. It varies a lot depending on where you reside, your circumstances, and your job. Still, suppose you're in the United Kingdom or the United States, where the median kind of average salary is somewhere around $50,000 something. In that case, I'm not then dipping into pending your circumstances. Still, getting $10,000 stashed away in savings is not that difficult. The situation is different if you're trying to provide for a family of 15 people on a budget of $50,000. If you are back to being a single person? Although it is unique, I will give this perhaps a three out of five-star rating for how tough it is to earn one hundred dollars every month. It is quite tough to save a total of $10,000 if you reside in a nation like India, where the average yearly salary is only $3,600. This makes it very hard to save money altogether.

Maintenance

How difficult is it to keep it going once you've established this source of revenue? The difficulty of sustaining the revenue from a side hustle after it has been established is one of the factors that our evaluation matrix considers for the side hustle category. Because after you've received the money and you can basically simply set it and forget it, maintaining this isn't that difficult, therefore we're going to give it a rating of 1 out of 5 stars.

Investing in stocks and shares is a very easy way to make passive income, and here's an example from my own life: at the moment, The majority of the $360,000 in my stocks and shares portfolio, which I've been building since 2015, is invested in the S&P 500 index fund. There are other sources of passive income, but they require higher maintenance over time. Assuming a rough average of 10% a year, that average should be around $682 per week in purely passive income. Now, I can't be bothered to work at the actual inflation-adjusted returns for that, but if we assume a rough average of 10% a year, that average should be around $682 per week.

Starting a YouTube channel

This is an area in which I have much experience. This is where I instruct others on how to carry out activities of this nature. Now that we have our side hustle evaluation matrix let's utilize it to determine how difficult it is to create a channel on YouTube. I will give this a rating of 1 out of 5 stars since creating a channel on YouTube is rather simple. All that is required is to go to YouTube.com, click the "Create Channel" button, and then you can start adding videos by just capturing them on your phone and then uploading them.

It is a lot tougher to generate excellent video because generating good videos is how you develop on YouTube, but it is really easy to get started on YouTube.

Challenges

How difficult is it, in reality, to generate real money off of YouTube? This is the true question we need to ask ourselves, and we should be asking it now. What actions would be necessary to reach our objective of a monthly passive income of $100? To begin, you need one thousand subscribers and four thousand hours of view time before you can become eligible for revenue on YouTube. It took me 52 videos and six months to gain my first thousand subscribers on my YouTube channel. If we take a look at the averages, we can see that it takes more than 90 videos, on average, to get 1000 subscribers. You should be aware that beginning a YouTube channel with the intention of making money from it right away will be difficult. You know that is extremely unlikely to occur, given that it took me 52 videos and six months to reach that point. You need to be able to exert the necessary effort and keep at this activity for a very extended amount of time at least once every week. At the very least, for two years before you can anticipate receiving anything in return.

Let's assume you've reached your goal of 1,000 members and have accumulated

4,000 hours of watch time; how difficult would it be to generate $100 each month? There is a huge amount of variation in this. However, the amount of income generated by every thousand views on YouTube is around $2.00 on average. Let's imagine that, on average, you make $2.00 per thousand views; as a result, if you want to make $100 a month on YouTube, you need 50,000 views on your videos. If you produce one video every week and assume that your older videos are not receiving any traffic, then each video you produce must have around 12,500 views for it to be successful. The typical YouTube channel may anticipate that around 20% of their followers will equal the average view count for each video. It is reasonable to assume that 20% of your subscribers, or 12,500 people, will watch each of your videos if you have 62,000 members.

Also, assuming that you do not have any material that will be relevant for an extended period, you will need around 60,000 subscribers to make $100 every month. You make more than $100 per month before you have 60,000 members. I believe that when I had about 10,000 members, I was generating $100 per month in revenue. It was quite early on, but when it comes to analyzing how difficult it is to complete, I'm giving this a rating of four stars out of five for how challenging it is.

While creating a YouTube account and uploading videos is simple, it can be challenging to become successful in the platform's competitive environment. It is worthwhile and provides a very useful set of skills. It's very amazing, but it's quite difficult to make money from YouTube, even though it's incredibly enjoyable because you get to meet people from all over the Internet, you get to learn how to talk to a camera, how to shoot, and how to edit videos, and it's great.

Maintenance

How challenging is it to keep up? Getting the first thousand subscribers is a lot more difficult than keeping it growing. This is because once you have 1000 subscribers and your channel grows, you've landed on a formula that works, so maintaining it becomes easier than starting from scratch. Finally, in terms of the effort required to maintain it, getting the first thousand subscribers is much more difficult than keeping it growing.

As a result, we're going to assign the upkeep of a YouTube channel the equivalent of around two out of five stars in the evaluation matrix for passive revenue streams generated by side hustles. To give you an idea, it took me seventy videos before I started seeing any income from YouTube advertisements. The YouTube channel currently generates around $12,000 per month in passive revenue from YouTube commercials; however, this income is not passive because I continue to add new videos to the channel. The vast majority of the revenue from advertisements comes from older videos instead of those just published within the past month. Because of my YouTube channel and all of the people that support it, I now have a passive income of $12,000 per month, which works out to roughly $3000 per week.

There are more methods of monetizing YouTube, such as brand deals and the sale of merchandise and other types of products. Still, they don't count as passive income from YouTube, which is why I'm not putting this in this suggestion for a matrix that evaluates side hustles.

Starting a podcast

Beginning a podcast is one more way to get an income without active labor. This is often easier than beginning a channel on YouTube, but expanding a podcast is far more difficult than building a YouTube channel. This is because podcasts do not have an algorithm that is helping them grow. It may seem strange, but many podcasts successfully utilize YouTube as a distribution platform.

Challenges

How difficult is it to get a podcast up and to run?How difficult is it to get a podcast up and to run? One out of five stars once more because it is not difficult at all to launch a podcast. You may begin recording a podcast as soon as you go on anchor.FM; all you need is your phone, and you and your friends can take turns using it to record the podcast. You may utilize a website called Riverside.FM is an Angel investment company that I recently became a part of. Riverside makes it incredibly simple to record remote podcast interviews, and launching a podcast using Riverside is not difficult. To reiterate, this is not passive income because podcasters generate money by depending on brand partnerships as their primary source of revenue.

There is no YouTube out sentence for podcasts, so you need sponsorship or a brand deal to make any money through your podcast. However, according to statistics, you may anticipate earning around $18.00 for the 32nd ad in a podcast and $25 for the 62nd ad for every 1000 views or 1000 listens. These numbers are based on the frequency of playback of advertisements. You will need around 1000 downloads per episode if you have a weekly podcast, meaning you would have 4000 downloads a month. If you put a 62nd ad in there and charge $25 per thousand views, that would make you run about $100 a month if you had 1000 downloads per episode and four episodes. So if you want to make $100 monthly, then you need to assume that you have a stream of sponsors who are giving you that level of sponsorship deal based on your This raises the question, "How difficult is it to achieve one thousand downloads per month?" Getting 1,000 podcast downloads per month is much more difficult than 1,000 views on YouTube. This is because YouTube has a great deal of built-in distribution, which distinguishes it from podcasts; additionally, there are more people on YouTube than on podcasts. However, if we look at the statistics, we can see that only the top 20% of podcasts worldwide receive an average of more than 1000 downloads every episode. To give you an example, one of my friends began her podcast about five months ago, and on average, each episode of her podcast receives between 400 and 500 downloads. This is just one example. Her is not at all awful, especially considering that she began this endeavor five months ago and had no audience when she first began. Because she has just begun uploading videos about her podcast on YouTube and has just released season two, she did not have the unfair edge I did when I began my podcast. This is because she only recently launched season two of her podcast. That will greatly assist the podcast's expansion, and I am fairly certain that over the next six months, she will reach a stage where she can quite easily make $100 per month from her podcast.

Returning to our evaluation matrix for side businesses, I'm going to give starting a podcast, which received one out of five stars and requires a monthly income of $100, a rating of three out of five stars because it's challenging but not as challenging as, say, monetizing on YouTube, where there is a minimum threshold. I'll give that a three out of five stars because it's hard but not as hard as monetizing on YouTube, where you have this minimum threshold.

Maintenance

However, it is not truly passive income because you must continually produce podcast episodes to maintain the brand partnerships linked with that revenue. It is simpler to keep going once you've already gotten started, as is the case with most things; once you've found a formula that works, once you know how to be a podcaster, however, once you've stumbled onto a formula that works, once you know how to be a podcaster.

Consequently, if you ask me how well the podcast is maintained, I will give you two stars.

I'll use an instance from my personal experience; my brother and I host a podcast, and we generate roughly $625 per week in total revenue from the show, thanks to sponsor partnerships and membership fees.

Affiliate marketing

For people who wish to make money in their leisure time, being an affiliate marketer is a great option. When you participate in affiliate marketing, it implies that you are selling other people's items in exchange for a commission on the sales of those products. Now, it would appear that 48% of affiliate marketers worldwide earn $20,000 a year, equivalent to $1660 each month, which is not at all terrible. Affiliate marketing is often producing very positive results for its participants.

Challenges

How difficult is it to get things running? This receives a rating of 2 stars out of a possible 5. Signing up for an affiliate program like Thomas and Associates is all you must do. So Amazon has its affiliate network, which I believe is probably the largest one in the world. Once you have your good links, you can publish them on your website, Twitter, social media, or anywhere else you choose. Also, if customers buy the goods through your link or, more generally, if they buy anything through your link on Amazon, you will earn a small part of the sales. As a result, affiliate marketing is very simple to begin, although it does require some initial investment.

How difficult is it to make one hundred dollars a month?

To be honest, this is a rather challenging task. If you were trying to sell a product that cost $50 and you were earning a commission of 5% on it, that would be quite fantastic. Amazon does not provide nearly as much as 5%; it offers 2% or 3% or something like that. So let's suppose you had a product that you were trying to sell, and it cost $50. So if you had a product that was $50 that you were trying to sell and you were getting 5% Commission on it, that would be pretty good. Let's say that your typical conversion rate, which is the ratio of people who visit the thing to the number of people who buy the product after visiting the thing, is 1% (which is a pretty reasonable conversion rate). In that case, you would need 8,000 people to visit your website or whatever it is that you have to make $100 every month. It is, in fact, pretty challenging to attract 8,000 visitors to your website for a certain product page. To be profitable in affiliate marketing, you must invest a lot of time and effort in the beginning, either to create an audience or to get enough domain authority in the industry you want to work in to attract visitors more easily.

Aside from Amazon, I am a part of just a few other affiliate programs. One of them is Skillshare, which has an intriguing affiliate scheme. If you refer someone to join up for a free trial on Skillshare, you are eligible to receive $7 in affiliate commission only for that one thing. Therefore, if you wanted to make $100 a month from affiliates, you would need 15 individuals to join Skillshare monthly using your affiliate link. This would bring your monthly total to $1,000. The question we need to ask is, how hard is it to acquire 15 new individuals to join up each month with your affiliate link? It's not that hard if you already have an audience, and it's not that difficult if you already have your lessons on Skillshare, as I have. I now have about nine of those.

How difficult is it to generate one hundred dollars per month to get back to our evaluation grid for the best side hustles? I will give this a rating of 3.5 stars because, once again, you need an audience. As I always say, you build an audience by creating useful content, releasing it once a week for free on the Internet, and continuing to do this for at least two years. I will give this a rating of 3.5 stars because, once again, you need an audience. If you only follow those three steps, I can promise that you will have an audience and that you will be able to generate some type of money from this passive income thing, but achieving this level of success may be pretty challenging. Once you've created it and once you start making money from affiliates, it's quite easy to maintain because, if you have Evergreen content, the sort that isn't relying on like current affairs or the latest news, people might search for over a long period, so we'll give that a rating of 3.5 stars. However, the good news is that once you've created it and started making money from affiliates, it's quite easy to maintain because once you. This becomes a form of passive income that can be considered reasonably acceptable.

Now, if we look at my business, which is based on Skillshare, we generate around $11,000 per month. That is sufficient money, which averages approximately $2750 per week. From Amazon, it comes to about $450 per month from the Amazon U.K. shop, with a little more coming from the Amazon stores in the United States and Canada.

Selling digital products

Selling digital things is one way to earn income without actively doing anything. These are one-time creations you make, such as an ebook, a download, an application, or something along those lines. You just need to produce it once to start making money off it, and then you may resell it an unlimited number of times because selling digital items typically does not incur further costs. This guy called Trust, who I follow on Twitter, created an iOS 14 icon set and sold it for around $30 a pop a few months ago. Due to the overwhelming demand for his icon pack, I believe he ultimately earned over $300,000 in a short period of time. This is a really good example. Therefore, he put a lot of effort into producing the pack, and now he is making a lot of money from selling it. Another illustration of this is my buddy Oliver from YouTube, who, according to him, has made $700,000 since 2014 by selling the Tumblr themes he designed for websites. It's fantastic that he's produced the website designs for Tumblr excellently and has made an average of $700,000 since 2014 across the board in total earnings.

Challenges

Because everyone is capable of writing a book, and any book may be considered a digital product, I will give this a grade of two stars out of a possible five. It is important to remember that the transaction of money represents an exchange of values; therefore, the thing you are selling must provide sufficient value to compensate and make up for the price you are selling it for. This can be challenging, particularly if you do not have any prior experience in dealing with transactions of this kind.

How difficult is it to make one hundred dollars a month?

Because the market for this kind of content is so competitive, you need to be genuinely good at what you do to convince people to buy your ebook, icon set, app, or website themes. Creating an ebook is relatively simple, but convincing people to buy it is a completely different challenge altogether. You may convince people to give you money for anything by determining a problem they are experiencing, then providing a solution to that problem, and finally charging them money for the service. If you can do those three things, making $100 a month won't be difficult for you at all. It is not impossible to make $100 every month; all you need is something that can alleviate a problem that other people are experiencing and that they are prepared to pay for.

Therefore, we will offer this a rating of 3 stars out of a possible 5 to make $100 each month selling things.

Maintenance

How difficult is it to keep up with? We will rate this as a two out of a possible five stars because, in most cases, you will be required to perform some level of product maintenance; nevertheless, it is typically far simpler to perform product maintenance than create a product from scratch.

Creating an online course

Making an online course is one way to generate passive revenue for yourself over time. Because this book is so lengthy, it could have been a complete online course had it been presented in video format. Online courses often use that medium.

How difficult is it to get things going?
We are going to give the first difficulty of creating an online course a rating of 2 out of 5 stars since it is not that tough to create an online course, but in general, you do need to know how to produce video; so sure, you truly could film an online course on your mobile device,

regardless of the phone that you're using. It is not difficult to create one, but to make $100 a month from it; your course needs to be truly good. This is because people will only pay for it if the course is good.

Using a service such as Skillshare won't have to worry about collecting fees from your students for your online classes. On Skillshare, I teach a huge number of classes. Since September of this year, I've been instructing on Skillshare, and I've just launched a brand new online class called Productivity for Creators, which is about how to launch a profitable side hustle. In this section of the guide, I'll explain how you may establish a side business in your free time without leaving your job. I pay for Skillshare, and I've been paying for it for years, even after I start teaching on it, since it's truly an amazing place to learn new things. The yearly Skillshare premium membership includes a pretty excellent bargain. They provide hundreds of lessons on a wide variety of subjects. Still, you should check out mine because most of the books and classes I've uploaded are focused on time management and other aspects of productivity.

Because you can teach things on Skillshare without explicitly needing to charge for them, it is a wonderful location to teach things, which is why I enjoy placing my courses on Skillshare. You can find more information here if you are interested in teaching on Skillshare. One of the many advantages of using Skillshare is that it functions similarly to YouTube and that anybody may publish a cluster. It is a lot simpler to use Skillshare if it meets certain quality standards, as opposed to having to develop your website and create your course platform and all the other things involved in doing so. We'll give this a rating of 2 out of 5 stars because it's relatively simple to get started.

Challenges

How difficult is it to make one hundred dollars a month? This is rather open to debate. If you want to follow the path of Skillshare, then you will need around 1700 minutes of watch time, equivalent to 28 hours of watch time, to make $100 each month using Skillshare. Therefore, if you provide a one-hour session on Skillshare, you will need around 28 students to sign up for that class each month and a bullet premium membership to make approximately one hundred dollars per month. At the very least, those are based on actual life figures accumulated for about two years on Skillshare.

How difficult is it to get 28 individuals to watch your class monthly? It shouldn't be too difficult to attract 28 people to attend your lesson every month if it's genuinely fairly excellent, which it seems like it is. If you already have an audience, it will be easy to get 28 people to view it monthly. This is because people will hopefully already know, like, and trust you, and because of this, they will watch your content and give you a shot because you have already built up that goodwill with them. To reiterate, one of the positive aspects of Skillshare as a platform is that it has its algorithm, which allows for the best content to come to the top. Even if you don't have an audience, there is a good chance that many people will recommend your class and give it a high rating if it is a good class and people watch it on Skillshare. This is true even if you don't have an audience. If you have a really good class and put it on Skillshare, read on. It will move to the top of the list and begin to be suggested to users who discover it on the homepage of Skillshare or who search for it directly.

The second approach to make $100 a month from a course is to just charge $100 for the course, and if you do that, all you need is one sale every single month to make that much money. How difficult would it be to sell a course to one new student per month? Now, if it's to your advantage, you're aware that the field of online education is rapidly expanding on an annual basis. Especially in light of everything going on with the epidemic, people are spending more and more money on online schooling. Therefore, if you possess an important ability that you can pass on to others, I believe that offering classes are one of the finest and easiest ways to do so. You don't need that many technical skills like making a website or anything like that; just shove it on Skillshare, and then people can take your course and learn on the Internet, which is cool overall. Well, what are the best ways to make passive income because it's fun to create a course you can teach stuff? You don't need that many technical skills like making a website or anything like that; just shove it on Skillshare. The positive aspect is that once you've completed the training and you've reached the point where you're making $100 per month from it, keeping your earnings at that level is fairly simple. As a result, we have decided to award it 2 out of a possible five stars. This is due to the fact that it is not always necessary to update the course; rather, you may do it on an ad hoc basis. You only need to make sure that you are receiving a respectable quantity of traffic to it, and you should keep working toward increasing that traffic over time.

These days, most of my online courses, or at least the ones that generate the most passive revenue, are housed on Skillshare. It's ludicrous, but the courses generate about $60,000 to $65,000 per month in solely passive money. I essentially do nothing for my Skillshare lessons once I've built them other than react to comments and occasionally mention them in videos, and that's like $60,000 a month in passive money for me. Those are just a few examples. What this translates to is that I bring in around $15,000 per week, which accounts for the vast majority of the passive income of $27,000 that this company earns every week.

Creating paid membership or community model

Creating some form of paid membership or community model can also be an effective strategy for earning passive money. This can be done in any color. This is a terrible idea in almost every circumstance unless you already have an audience you regularly interact with. Everything gets much simpler if you have an established following, which you can do by continually producing material that has shown to be of high value over a protracted period. That audience knows, likes, and trusts you, so when you say, "hey folks, join up on my Patreon," it is probable that some people will sign up for it.

The second method for establishing a membership is to develop a value proposition that is so alluring that individuals will be prepared to pay money for the privilege of participating in a community-based activity. Suppose we use my buddy Hannah, a YouTuber, as an example. In that case, she has over 600,000 followers on YouTube, and the last time I looked, she had approximately 626 patrons supporting her channel on Patreon. This indicates that if we look at her Patreon stats, which are public, she is making somewhere between 3,000 and

5,000 pounds or about 3,000 and $7000 per month in passive income from this audience; however, it's only about 600 people out of a total audience of 600,000, which means that only one in 1000 of her subscribers have signed up to her Patreon. You must be aware that for Patreon to generate a considerable amount of revenue requires a sizable audience. If those statistics are accurate elsewhere, including Kathmandu Bellows Patron, you must have a large following. Again, this somewhat depends on the price you set for them and the specific value you offer.

My buddy, Laura, owns a website known as fewer slums and has a premium membership community that costs $5 per month. This community is an additional illustration of a paid neighborhood or neighborhood association membership. She began doing this in the summer of 2019, and at the time, she had no audience. She simply posted one hundred blog entries over one hundred working days to build an audience. As a result, when she offered membership in March 2020, she already had some paying members. I believe she reached the $100,000 mark in yearly recurring income about a month ago, which is quite amazing for something that started less than two years ago.

Challenges

How challenging is it to get a membership program off the ground? It's not hard at all. Because it is so simple to get started on your own, we will award this a rating of one star. You need to sign up for a membership site of some type, like Patreon, and create an account there.

How difficult is it to make one hundred dollars a month?

In order to make $100 every month, you need to deliver $100 per month's worth of value to your customers, which is a challenging goal to achieve. So, we'll give that a rating of 4 out of 5, but the good news is that once you've perfected the formula and are now making $100 per month, it's much easier to keep it up. This is because the way the economics of membership communities work is that provided you keep showing up and providing value you know people have already signed up for, you'll be able to keep making money from them. It shouldn't be too difficult for you to keep up the degree of assistance that you are giving to them.

With regard to this company, we offer a membership community to our former students of our part-time YouTuber Academy, and the revenue that we generate each week from this membership community comes to around $2800. It is not a very passive activity since we run like three or four events per week in addition to like twice a day co-working events on zoom, and we have a lot of other stuff going on; thus, it requires a lot of labor. A weekly income of around $2,800 is considered to be rather successful in the membership group.

Creating a business that sells goods and services and then automating that business

This is the kind of material that Tim Ferris discusses at length in his book "The Four-Hour Workweek," in which he explains that there are a great many businesses that you could start, sell products or services for, and then delegate, outsource, and automate in smart ways in order to make the income passive. So, to continue using my friend Ali as an example, I'll say that Ali discusses his one-million-dollar Shopify shop on his YouTube channel. He creates, manufactures, and distributes a variety of beautiful vegan leather workplace accessories such as purses, mouse pads, and other items. This required a significant amount of effort and setup, but now that he has a team of three other people to operate the firm, he spends far less of his time doing so. Even while he does spend around ten hours each week maintaining things, he may consider this a form of passive income because it brings in a consistent amount.

My buddy operates a marketing business that specializes in Facebook and Instagram ads. He has clients who pay him a few hundred dollars each month to handle their advertisements on Facebook and Instagram. When he first sets up the advertising on Facebook and Instagram, he just needs to put in a modest bit of effort, but after that, everything is more or less automatic, and he has a crew supporting him. Because he has automated several facets of that company with the help of tools like ZAP, he just needs to put in a negligible amount of effort each month to ensure that it continues to function normally.

So, all of these are distinct methods to generate passive income from some type of business that provides an item or service; yet, it is extremely challenging to get started with any of these things. To begin things rolling, we're going to give this a grade of four out of five stars since, once more, you need to construct a business, which is fairly difficult to make, particularly the kinds of businesses that actually bring value.

Challenges

How difficult is it to make one hundred dollars a month? Equally, we're going to give it a rating of four out of five stars for making one hundred dollars per month since you have to be able to deliver value, and it's difficult to produce value. It is not as simple as creating an account and beginning a platform by simply depositing some money in it. You have to actively help other people, which might be challenging, but the good news is that once you've gotten started with anything, upkeep will be a little bit simpler. This is true for all endeavors. Therefore, we are going to award that a grade of three stars out of five for its upkeep.

Building apps or websites

Building an app, website, or other kinds of a software product that you can sell either as a one-time purchase or, more likely in today's market, as a subscription service is one of the most effective ways to generate passive income. In fact, a whole subcategory is devoted to this business model, and it is known as SAS (software as a service). There are hundreds of examples of people who have built software businesses that are making passive income. They share their revenue numbers, tell you how they got started, and also give you their tips on the website indiehackers.com. Now, if you look at this website, you will see that some people have built software businesses that are making passive income. In point of fact, I was just featured in an interview on an episode of the Indie Hackers podcast, which is extremely great because I've been following both the show and the website for years. During the course of the conversation, the topic of launching an online school comparable to the part-time YouTuber Academy came up.

Since I've got some hands-on experience with this topic, while I was still in school, I created a website called bement ninja and another one called U.K. cat ninja that offered software as a service. It was a question bank for medical applicants applying to medical school to help them do well in the admissions exams, and this was something that my brother and I programmed totally from scratch. The bank intended to assist medical applicants in doing well in admissions and tests. We were taught this when we were younger, and as a result, we put forth a lot of effort throughout the summer of 2015 to ensure that these things took place. I believe that in year one, we made around $10,000 through bement ninja, and in year five, the amount we made was approximately $25,000 last year. It was a lot of work to get these things up and running, but they are bringing in a decent amount of money now.

When it comes to getting started, I'm going to give this a perfect score of five stars because developing an app is a challenging endeavor in and of itself. You not only need to be able to develop it, but you also need to know how to code, be able to provide something appealing to give customers and be able to do so. Although it requires a lot of effort and may be quite challenging, this activity is a lot of fun.

Challenges

How difficult is it to make one hundred dollars a month? I'm going to give the difficulty of making $100 per month a grade of four stars due to the fact that it's simple to create an app, but it's a whole other challenge to convince users to pay for the app. Therefore, we are going to award that a rating of 4 stars. We are going to award that a grade of three stars since one positive aspect shared by all aspects is that they are less difficult to maintain.

Check out my other books, which I've written about how to become an entrepreneur, how I started creating my businesses from scratch, and how I learned to code.

Reasons many struggle at building streams of passive income

Nowadays, it seems as if passive income streams are being discussed wherever I turn: why you should start them, which ones you should start, how they may improve your life, and how much money you can earn from them.

In order to work less and yet live the lifestyle they choose or, more often, to give up medicine completely, doctors often search for methods to generate passive income. Many of these same professionals have discovered; however, that passive income is not as simple to get by as everyone claims.

I'm here to inform you that it's not always simple; else, everyone would have amassed enormous passive income streams. Despite having the best of hopes, the majority fall short of their objectives for a number of reasons. In terms of my own passive income sources, I'm still not where I want to be, and I'm always trying to figure out why.

Do any of these reasons for why you aren't generating the passive income you desire ring a bell?

1. Anxiety of failing

Success is defined as moving from failure to failure without losing motivation. — William Churchill

"I haven't blown it. I just discovered 10,000 methods that won't work. Theodore Edison

You could not be generating passive income streams due to a strong fear of failure, which is another major factor. You avoid attempting new things because you're terrified of failing. Instead, you continue to behave in the same old ways, and your inaction ensures that nothing changes.

It may seem contradictory, but the secret to conquering your fear of failure is to keep failing until it has less of an impact on you. You must understand that failure merely advances your progress toward your objective. Yes, we all strive for perfection and are used to being at the top of our courses. Most likely, you haven't failed at many things in your life. Realize that some amount of failure is probably inevitable when it comes to passive income sources, but that you will learn from each setback, and that will eventually help you succeed.

2. Setting up the incorrect passive income source

I'm sorry to tell you, but if your present passive income stream isn't producing, it may not be the right one for you. One of the hardest decisions to make is whether to keep trying, hoping that a little more perseverance would help you get through, or whether to move on.

Flexibility and resourcefulness are just as important as commitment and perseverance. Part of the trip is figuring out what works and what doesn't. Never hesitate to take a step back and figure out why something isn't working. Obtain guidance from mentors. Even elite athletes have coaches to assist them in resolving problems.

Analyze your motivation for doing it in the first place. Is it only because you believed it would bring in money, or are you really enthusiastic about it? In my perspective, neither is incorrect, but over time, if you do not see the desired outcomes, it will be difficult to keep continuing if you're not enthusiastic about it.

3. Not working hard enough

You've just begun your road toward creating a passive income stream. To go where you want to go, you must continually course correct along the route, particularly initially. In the 10x Rule, Grant Cardone says it best: "You must establish aims that are ten times what you believe you desire and then do ten times what you think it would take to achieve those targets. Tremendous action must be preceded by massive contemplation. Do you really put in 10 times the effort, or are you only making an effort to survive?

The secret to success in this endeavor is to devote a significant amount of time and effort to concentrate on your passive income sources, particularly at first. As I've already said, passive income doesn't always mean not working at all. It involves investing the majority of your time and effort in the beginning, and the benefits keep accruing over time.

Ask yourself whether you are putting in the required effort to maintain the health and direction of your passive income enterprise. Your initial level of effort and your level of intelligence also have an impact on your success.

4. Customers

Anyone pursuing a passive income company with the incorrect emphasis forgets about their clients. Customers want to feel cared for; therefore, you need to establish that type of trust. They want to know that you care about them and that teaching makes you happy. It helps to create your authority and credibility by demonstrating to them your faith in your service and company.

Your audience will turn to someone who is committed to the long term as soon as they suspect you aren't. And they'll notice those sensations right away.

If you're merely making a little effort, you won't be able to convince people to believe in whatever you have to give. It will be obvious if your motivation is just to make a fast buck. Additionally, if you don't really believe in your goods, your customers won't either.

Additionally, without clients, no one will be available to purchase what you are offering. To keep customers coming back for more, you need to have a devoted following of individuals who trust you and your business. Without it, no company can be successful.

5. Competition

There are other players in the game besides you. In order to remain in the game, successful company owners keep up with their rivals. They must be aware of emerging trends and the factors that influence consumer brand loyalty. They must do a study on their own items to determine the factors that influence purchasing (or discourage them). It takes continual analysis, changes to your websites and products, time for high-level thinking, and everyday maintenance effort to stay relevant.

In all honesty, the labor never ends. Most business owners should stay current with their industry and competitors, but if you're off pretending that your company can function without you while still generating millions, you've probably forgotten about other people altogether.

6. Expansion

Realistic passive income companies are successful because their owners have worked out how to increase production by adding skilled, talented team members to their organization. You won't be able to maintain your team, or you won't even employ one from the start if you're continuously on vacation at the beach, never checking in, and leaving your staff to do all the work.

A group that works effectively together is one that is led by a committed, conscientious, and caring individual. Your employees won't be enthusiastic or present if you aren't, and your company won't develop.

What it takes to create passive income business

People who dedicate their professions to creating passive revenue streams for their businesses are everywhere on the internet. Although there is endless commercial potential, I don't believe that everyone who tries will be successful.

What therefore is required to establish a passive income stream? Here are a few items I think you should have.

1. The right mindset

You've undoubtedly guessed by now that having the appropriate mentality is the most important need for creating a successful passive income company. Make sure your incentives are focused on adding value for your customers before you launch any form of company.

Do you solely want to make money from this? Do you solely have your own interests in mind? Are you attempting to shift all the burden to someone else while keeping all the credit for yourself? If so, you won't be a successful company owner who generates passive revenue.

To create a viable passive income company, see significant development, and generate real money, you must:

- Arrive with the intention of giving your clients value.

- Desire to do the hard labor in the trenches (not permanently, but certainly in the beginning).

- Have a desire to see your clients develop and learn from what you have to give.

- Have such a strong commitment to your subject that you live and breathe it.

Customers will detect a false in you and flee if you don't have that value-centered, customer-loving, enthusiastic perspective about your profession.

2. Good work ethic

There is no such thing as instant success; thus, you must consistently present yourself. Every successful passive income venture has years of audience development, failed products, and steady but sluggish growth to its credit. Successful, practical company owners who rely on passive revenue are aware of this and are ready to put in a lot of effort—and by a lot, I mean a lot of work.

The techniques and tools that enable you to generate passive income were built with a tremendous lot of effort and dedication. And those who initially had that ambition and determination often do not "rest on their laurels" after the money begins rolling in. — *Mariah Carey*

3. Scalability

If you want to build a viable passive income company, there is one thing you must be good at beyond your character, work ethic, and actual goods.

I'm referring to scalability.

You need to employ a strong staff and then build up the correct mechanisms to automate the job for you if you want your firm to thrive while still allowing you to walk away from being entirely hands-on.

By assigning daily duties to team members and automating procedures, all successful passive income company owners have learned how to utilize their time in order to expand their audience and provide more value to more people.

The proverbial "number of checks they're willing to sign" is what separates a six-figure company owner from a seven-figure business owner.

And your email marketing is a reliable way to automate.

Conclusion

Although the provision of one's services in order to generate income is how businesses are run, it is always preferable to have income coming from a variety of sources so that you can remain solvent even if one of your income streams dries up. This allows you to continue operating even if you lose one of your revenue streams.

If you enjoyed this book and are interested in beginning your own journey toward generating passive income online and becoming an entrepreneur. If you liked this book, you should also check out my other books. I want to offer my sincere gratitude for reading this, and I hope to see you in the next book. Bye!

www.ingramcontent.com/pod-product-compliance
Lightning Source LLC
Chambersburg PA
CBHW070244220526
45465CB00004B/1515